D0498149

THE NASTIEST THINGS EVER SAID ABOUT REPUBLICANS

THE

NASTIEST THINGS

EVER SAID
ABOUT
REPUBLICANS

Collected and Edited by

Martin Higgins

THE LYONS PRESS
Guilford, Connecticut
An imprint of the Globe Pequot Press

The Lyons Press is an imprint of The Globe Pequot Press.

10 9 8 7 6 5 4 3 2 1

Printed in the United States of America

Designed by Carol Sawyer/Rose Design

ISBN 10: 1-59228-839-1

ISBN 13: 978-1-59228-839-7

Library of Congress Cataloging-in-Publication Data is available on file.

This book is dedicated to Patrick Joseph Higgins, football player,
devoted coach of Pop Warner teams, live improvisational wild man,
the consummate Curly he strove to be, and a brother who set aside our differences
and grudges years before he died. If I told a joke, he could top it.
When I worked out a complex routine, he could reinterpret it instantly and perform
it effortlessly—while laying his audience on the floor. He was the Natural.

Contents

INTRODUCTION

*T*his book, along with its evil twin, *The Nastiest Things Ever Said About Democrats*, neatly carves the American political system into two relatively house-trained animals: the Republican/Conservative/Right and the Democrat/Liberal/Left.

Back in the seventies, Senator S. I. Hayawaka, (D-CA) made this helpful distinction between both major parties: "Republicans are people who, if you were drowning fifty feet from shore, would throw you a twenty-five-foot rope and tell you to swim the other twenty-five feet because it would be good for your character. Democrats would throw you a hundred-foot rope and then walk away looking for other good deeds to do."

Like Groucho Marx once said, "All people are born alike—except Republicans and Democrats."

America's political divide has deepened in recent years. The partisan mood is hostile and increasingly polarized. It's become an Uncivil

War. Sound and fury, indeed. It's 24-7 invective, with rants and name-calling fueled by every conceivable media orifice.

With this collection, I hope to further inflame these emotions as well as buttress the cause of prejudice and proud identity. Make this book your go-to source for quotes about Republicans. It will come in handy whenever you're going up against your right-wing adversaries. Choose a zinger. Let the quotes fly, and stand back. Good luck on the political battlefield.

MARTIN HIGGINS
DENVER, COLORADO
JULY 2006

In this world of sin and sorrow, there is always something to be thankful for. As for me, I rejoice that I am not Republican.

—*H. L. Mencken*

Oh no, the dead have risen and they're voting Republican!

—*Lisa Simpson,* The Simpsons

THE
NASTIEST THINGS
EVER SAID
ABOUT
REPUBLICANS

WE STILL HAVE NIXON TO KICK AROUND

IF NIXON DID NOT EXIST, it would be necessary for Americans to invent him. He's the Mount Rushmore of failed presidential ambitions. More than being an awkward caricature of a jowly, sweaty politician, Nixon fought furiously against an imagined tide of opposition as a way of life.

His enemies reveled in his blatant dishonesties. By the time of his second term in the White House, the nation had grown all too familiar with his stilted body language, the forced gestures, and insincere facial expressions. He gave lying a bad name.

Although a great many of us celebrated his self-inflicted downfall, he nonetheless paved the way for future Republican con men to become president. They just knew how to lie and play the media game better than Tricky Dick.

I don't think the son of a bitch knows the difference between truth and lying.

—*President Harry S. Truman*

Did you know Richard Nixon is the only president whose formal portrait was painted by a police sketch artist?

—Tonight Show *host Johnny Carson*

When I first began this campaign, I just wanted to beat Nixon. Now I want to save the country from him.

—*John F. Kennedy, during the 1960 presidential campaign*

Avoid all needle drugs. The only dope worth shooting is
Richard Nixon.

—Sixties activist Abbie Hoffman

Nixon was just venal. He didn't realize how evil he was.

—artist Ralph Steadman

Nixon bleeds people. He draws every drop of blood and then drops
them from a cliff. He'll blame any person he can put his foot on.

—Martha Mitchell, wife of Attorney General John Mitchell

Nixon was the most notorious liar in the country.

—FBI director J. Edgar Hoover

If ever there was a man ill-suited by his own nature for the full and relentless exposure of national politics, the fierce give and take, it is Richard Nixon.

—author David Halberstam

Richard Nixon impeached himself. He gave us Gerald Ford as his revenge.

—Representative Bella Abzug

Nixon was brought down by people who were a hell of a lot worse than he was.

—*former Nixon speechwriter Pat Buchanan*

I sent my flowers across the hall to Mrs. Nixon, but her husband remembered what a Democrat I am and sent them back.

—*actress Bette Davis*

If Nixon is alone in a room, is anyone there?

—*feminist Gloria Steinem*

I wouldn't trust Nixon from here to that phone.

—*Senator Barry Goldwater*

History buffs probably noted the reunion at a Washington party
a few weeks ago of three ex-presidents: Carter, Ford, and Nixon—
See No Evil, Hear No Evil, and Evil.

—*Senator Robert J. Dole*

Well, if you give me two weeks . . .

—*President Dwight D. Eisenhower, when asked to sum up
the contribution of Vice President Richard Nixon*

The Eichmann trial taught the world the banality of evil; now Nixon is teaching the world the banality of evil.

—journalist I. F. Stone

⌒

[Nixon] was like a kamikaze pilot who keeps apologizing for the attack.

—columnist Mary McGrory in 1962

⌒

You won't have Nixon to kick around anymore, because, gentlemen, this is my last press conference.

—Richard M. Nixon, after losing the election for governor of California in 1962

⌒

A foul caricature of himself, a man with no soul, no inner
convictions, with the integrity of a hyena and the style of a
poison toad.

—writer Hunter S. Thompson

I am a fan of President Nixon. I worship the quicksand he walks on.

—humorist Art Buchwald

Nixon is the kind of politician who would cut down a redwood tree,
then mount the stump for a speech on conservation.

—Senator Adlai Stevenson

Sir Richard-the-Chicken-Hearted.

—Vice President Hubert H. Humphrey

I may not know much, but I know chicken shit from chicken salad.

—President Lyndon B. Johnson, referring to a Nixon speech

Nixon was so crooked that he needed servants to help him screw his pants on every morning.

—Hunter S. Thompson

A real middle-class uneducated swindler with all the virtues of a seller of fountain-pens in Naples.

> —*British journalist John Calmann, on President Nixon*

Nixon is a shifty-eyed goddamn liar. He's one of the few in the history of this country to run for high office talking out of both sides of his mouth at the same time and lying out of both sides.

> —*President Harry S. Truman*

Nixon couldn't take his top advisors to China. They were all too busy making license plates.

> —*comic Jack Carter*

If he wants to do his country a favor, he'll stay over there.
—*Senator Barry Goldwater, on Nixon's trip to China*

The essence of Richard Nixon is loneliness.
—*Secretary of State Henry A. Kissinger*

It was a Greek tragedy. Nixon was fulfilling his own nature. Once it started, it could not end otherwise.
—*Henry A. Kissinger*

Here is a guy who's had a stake driven through his heart. I mean, really nailed to the bottom of the coffin with a wooden stake, and a silver bullet through the forehead for good measure—and yet [Nixon] keeps coming back.

—ABC News reporter Ted Koppel in 1984

Just when you think there's nothing to write about, Nixon says, "I am not a crook."

—Art Buchwald

Nixon's motto was: If two wrongs don't make a right, try three.

—author Norman Cousins

He inherited some good instincts from his Quaker forebears, but by diligent hard work, he overcame them.

—*columnist James Reston*

When the cold light of history looks back on Richard Nixon's five years of unrestrained power in the White House, it will show you that he had the same effect on conservative/Republican politics as Charles Manson and the Hell's Angels had on hippies and flower power.

—*Hunter S. Thompson*

II

REAGAN
REMEMBERED

WITH HIS HONEYED VOICE, President Ronald Wilson Reagan was revered as The Great Communicator. He perfectly understood the mike and camera. He took direction well from media handlers such as Roger Ailes (the man behind the curtain at Fox News).

As president, Reagan adopted a John Wayne swagger from his Hollywood days. That tough, aw-shucks demeanor appealed to Middle America. He rode high in the POTUS saddle. He mocked the Soviet Union; he infuriated Democrats with his blithe disregard of facts; and he always managed to be a good sport—even after he was shot!

He was pure Teflon. Scandals like Iran-Contra slid right off his jocular, sunny exterior. He was the anti-Nixon. He symbolized the new epoch of GOP domination and eponymous Reagan Democrats.

Throughout his presidential reign, Reagan's leading lady, the iron-fisted Nancy, ran interference for him. Behind his twinkly, crinkly, optimistic facade always lurked Mommy Dearest.

Washington could not tell a lie; Nixon could not tell the truth;
Reagan cannot tell the difference.

—*satirist Mort Sahl*

Reagan is the triumph of the embalmer's art.

—*author Gore Vidal*

I believe that Ronald Reagan will someday make this country what it
once was . . . an arctic wilderness.

—*comic Steve Martin*

I think Nancy does most of his talking; you'll notice that she never drinks water when Ronnie speaks.

comic Robin Williams

In the heat of a political lifetime, Reagan innocently squirrels away tidbits of misinformation and then, sometimes years later, casually drops them into his public discourse, like gumballs in a quiche.

—reporter Lucy Howard

The battle for the mind of Ronald Reagan was like the trench warfare of World War I. Never have so many fought so hard for such barren terrain.

—*White House speechwriter and columnist Peggy Noonan*

People say satire is dead. It's not dead; it's alive and living in the White House. Reagan makes a Macy's Thanksgiving Day float look ridiculous. I think he's slowly but surely regressing into movies again. In his mind he's looking at dailies, playing dailies over and over.

—*Robin Williams*

I know for a fact that Mr. Reagan is not clear about the difference between the Medici and the Gucci. He knows that Nancy wears one.

—*Gore Vidal*

Ronald Reagan Bra: supports the right and ignores the left.

— *graffiti*

President Ronald Reagan won because he ran against Jimmy Carter. If he had run unopposed, he would have lost.

—*Mort Sahl*

Ronald Reagan just signed the new tax law. But I think he was in Hollywood too long. He signed it, "Best wishes, Ronald Reagan."

—*Johnny Carson*

Nancy Reagan fell down and broke her hair.

—*Johnny Carson*

Ronnie's hero is Calvin Coolidge and Nancy's is Calvin Klein.

—*comic Bob Hope*

Nancy Reagan is about as much fun as a sneeze in the middle of a piss.

—*comic David Feldman*

There is a power struggle going on between President Reagan's advisers. Moe and Curly are out. Larry is still in.

—*Johnny Carson*

Reagan's proof that there's life after death.

—*Mort Sahl*

It's our fault. We should have given him better parts.
>   —*Jack Warner, president of Warner Brothers Studios,*
>   *on accepting blame for Reagan winning*
>   *the 1980 presidential election*

California governor Reagan and I have one thing in common:
we both played football. I played for Michigan, he played for
Warner Brothers.

>   —*President Gerald Ford*

That would have been a great ticket, Reagan and Ford—an actor and
a stuntman.

>   —*Johnny Carson*

I am not disturbed by Ronald Reagan's Alzheimer's. You know, there's not a lot of cleaner pictures of karma in the world. I mean, it's not a very Christian way of thinking; I do stray sometimes. But I'll go right from him mocking the farm workers and eating grapes on television during the boycott to him dribbling. And I feel a sense of justice.

—actor Sean Penn

Ronald Reagan was the least knowledgeable president I ever met.

—Representative Thomas P. "Tip" O'Neill Jr.

You've got to be careful quoting Reagan because when you do it accurately it's called mudslinging.

—Democratic Party presidential nominee Walter Mondale in 1984

Reagan doesn't die his hair—he's just prematurely orange.

—*Vice President Gerald Ford*

Did you see President Reagan's press conference? They asked him fifteen questions. He got two right.

—*David Feldman*

III

AM-BUSHED: FATHER *AND* SON

IN THE CASE OF OUR FORTY-FIRST AND FORTY-THIRD PRESIDENTS, George Herbert Walker Bush and George Walker Bush, not only did Junior fall close to the family shrub, but he seems to have changed into a tumbleweed on the way down.

Saturday Night Live's Dana Carvey could flawlessly mimic Poppa Bush's slangy blab and arcane utterances, but no impersonator seems able to accurately capture W's limited vocabulary, cockeyed logic, and Rotary Club pancake breakfast delivery. The essence of Dubya is too maddeningly consistent to reduce into a comic act.

Dubya's critics often refer to his stumbling speeches and incurious nature as a sign of trenchant stupidity. That's too harsh of a label for the nation's first slacker-in-chief.

Prep schools and an Ivy League education were handy for him insofar as being places where the family Rolodex trumps critical thought or integrity. And so, this scion of wealth and privilege was born, bred, and groomed to ravage America.

The son wanted to avenge and upstage his father in Iraq. If only the younger Bush had remained a functional drunk in dusty Midland, Texas, and stayed out of politics altogether . . .

George W. Bush is not like Hitler. Hitler was elected.

—*comic Patton Oswalt*

Now, I don't want to get off on a rant here, but as a comedian, with George W. Bush coming into office, I feel like the owner of a hardware store before a hurricane.

—*comic Dennis Miller in* 2000

President George W. Bush is going on his annual vacation. The
White House says he goes to his Texas ranch to unwind. I'm
thinking, when does he wind?

—David Letterman, on the Late Show
with David Letterman

You are a donkey. You're an alcoholic, Mr. Danger, or rather, you're
a drunkard.

—Venezuelan president Hugo Chavez,
on President George W. Bush

Read my lips: No new promises.

—Johnny Carson, on President George H. W. Bush

Some Democrats say the estimated $60 billion cost of a war with Iraq could be better spent at home. When he heard that, President Bush agreed and announced plans to bomb Ohio.

—*Jay Leno in 2003*

George W. Bush promised a small government. But only because he's incapable of running a big one.

—*comic Randy Harken*

Since the [George W.] Bush administration is basically a monarchy, he should pass the crown to Jenna. She couldn't do worse than this bunch of airheads and bullies.

—*columnist Maureen Dowd*

George W. Bush is as bright as an egg timer.

—comedian Chevy Chase

President George W. Bush met with the prime minister of Ireland, who gave him the traditional bowl of shamrocks. There was an awkward moment when President Bush said, "Where are the pink hearts and yellow moons?"

—Conan O'Brien, host of Late Night with Conan O'Brien

All I ask is that for once you guys stop seeing me as the son of George Bush.

—George W. Bush, speaking to a reporter while running for governor of Texas in 1994

George W. Bush has helped those who have most, hurt those who have least, and ignored everyone in between.

—General Wesley Clark

He's a cheap thug.

—musician John Mellencamp,
on President George W. Bush

I was taught that it was the Congress that makes the laws, and the president's supposed to sign them, and he's supposed to enforce them. He's not just supposed to make them up.

—Senator Russ Feingold, referring to
President George W. Bush, on The Daily Show

You get the feeling that if George W. Bush had been president during other periods in American history, he would have sided with the candle lobby against electricity, the buggy-makers against cars, and typewriter companies against computers.

—*Senator John Kerry*

George W. Bush giving tax cuts is like Jim Jones giving Kool-Aid. It tastes good but it'll kill you.

—*Reverend Al Sharpton*

At least in Vietnam George W. Bush had an exit strategy.

—*bumper sticker*

After trying not to emulate his father's presidency in any way, W. emulated it in the worst possible way. He came out of a conflict with Saddam as a towering figure with soaring approval ratings and ended up as a shrunken figure with scalding approval ratings.

—*Maureen Dowd*

If George W. Bush is given a second term, and retains a Republican Congress and a compliant federal judiciary, he and his allies are likely to embark on a campaign of political retribution the likes of which we haven't seen since Richard Nixon.

—*pundit Paul Begala in 2004*

George W. Bush says, "Gore's book needs a lot of explaining." Of course, Bush says that about every book.

—*comic Bill Maher, host of* Politically Incorrect

In the Clinton administration, we worried the president would open his zipper. In the Bush administration, they worry the president will open his mouth.

—*pundit James Carville*

I didn't vote for you, I didn't even think of voting for you, and I probably won't next time.

—*Robert Strauss, after being asked by President George H. W. Bush to be ambassador to Moscow*

George W. Bush is like a bad comic working the crowd. A moron, if you'll pardon the expression.

—*actor Martin Sheen*

[George W.] Bush pointed to positive signs in Iraq, like how the economy is taking off, thanks to a booming car bomb business.

—*comic Drew Carey*

The Clinton White House today said they would start to give national security and intelligence briefings to George W. Bush. I don't know how well this is working out. Today after the first one Bush said, "I've got one question: What color is the red phone?"

—*Bill Maher in late* 2000

To say Bush was a bit testy is like saying gravel is not as nutritious as it looks. He even snapped at [White House reporter] Helen Thomas. For crumb's sake, who snaps at Helen Thomas? It's like biting the head off a Smurf.

—comic *Will Durst*

President George W. Bush urged Middle Eastern countries to modernize, saying "modernization is not the same as Westernization." And then, mentally exhausted, he collapsed into a chair.

Jimmy Fallon, Saturday Night Live's *"Weekend Update"*

George W. Bush, this man is a war criminal, and we will see that he is brought to trial.

—*Mohammed Saeed al-Sahaf, aka "Baghdad Bob," the former Iraqi minister of information*

The difference between Osama bin Laden and George W. Bush is that one's a militant fundamentalist zealot who murders innocent people for his own religious and political agenda, and the other is Osama bin Laden.

—*photographer Dan Dion*

The Dalai Lama visited the White House and told the president that he could teach him to find a higher state of consciousness. Then after talking to Bush for a few minutes, he said, "You know what? Let's just grab lunch."

—Bill Maher

Oh, come on. That's like Hitler's dog loved him. That is the silliest reason.

—Bill Maher, after his talk-show guest Christopher Hitchens said it was to President Bush's credit that he got Laura Bush to marry him because "she's an absolutely extraordinary woman"

I'm not comparing Bush to Adolph Hitler, because George Bush, for one thing, is not as smart as Adolph Hitler.

—television actor David Clennon

A recent conversation: *Dubya*: "Look at the clock, time is racing!" *Cheney*: "That's the second hand, George."

—comic Dennis Miller

The emperor has no clothes. When are people going to face the reality? Pull this curtain back!

—House minority leader Nancy Pelosi, on President George W. Bush

[George W.] Bush is as stubborn as Slim Pickens in *Dr. Strangelove*: He'd rather ride Rummy to Armageddon than concede that Iraq was a botched project.

—reporter Howard Fineman

You know, a lot of people think George W. Bush is stupid, but I did some research and my SATs are much lower than the guy George paid to take his.

—David Feldman

As ballots continue to be counted, election officials in New Mexico now give George W. Bush a small lead in that state. Bush said he was surprised to be in the lead there since he spent so much time as governor trying to keep New Mexicans from entering the country in the first place.

—*Tina Fey*, Saturday Night Live's
"*Weekend Update*"*in* 2000

Wow. This goofy child president we have on our hands now. He is demonstrably a fool and a failure, and this is only the summer of '03.

—*Hunter S. Thompson*

President George W. Bush gave a rousing speech to the United Nations General Assembly. Afterward, in a touching show of support, every foreign dignitary shook hands with the president and smiled warmly as he mispronounced their names.

—*Tina Fey*, Saturday Night Live's *"Weekend Update"*

In Louisiana, President [George W.] Bush met with over 15,000 National Guard troops. Here's the weird part, nobody remembers seeing him there.

—*Craig Kilborn, host of the* Late Late Show

Senator John McCain recently compared the situation in Iraq to the Vietnam era—to which President George W. Bush replied, "What does Iraq have in common with drinking beer in Texas?"

—*Craig Kilborn*

[George W.] Bush said today he is being stalked. He said wherever he goes, people are following him. Finally, someone told him, "Psst, that's the Secret Service."

—*Jay Leno, host of the* Tonight Show

President [George W.] Bush gave his first-ever presidential radio address in both English and Spanish. Reaction was mixed, however, as people were trying to figure out which one was which.

—*Dennis Miller*

The president finally explained why he sat in that classroom on 9/11 for seven minutes after he was told the country was under attack. He said he was "collecting his thoughts." What a time to start a new hobby.

—*Bill Maher, on President George W. Bush*

Anyone who eats pork rinds can't be all good.

—former first lady Barbara Bush, on her husband

I married the first man I ever kissed. When I tell that to my children, they just about throw up.

—Barbara Bush

President [George W.] Bush said today he would like America to establish a permanent base on the moon. This is all part of his plan to get Americans used to an environment where the air is unbreathable and there are no trees.

—Jay Leno

If he can't run for office any better than he runs the Texas Rangers, he doesn't have an advantage.

—*Ed Martin, former executive director of Texas's Democratic Party, on George W. Bush's partial ownership of a major league baseball team*

You know if I had a nickel for every time Bush has mentioned 9/11, I could raise enough reward money to go after Bin Laden.

—*Jon Stewart, host of* The Daily Show

President [George W.] Bush announced we're going to Mars, which means he's given up on Earth.

—*Jon Stewart*

A pin-stripin', polo-playin', umbrella-totin' Ivy Leaguer, born with a silver spoon so far in his mouth that you couldn't get it out with a crowbar.

> —*Bill Baxley, lieutenant governor of Alabama in 1988, on President George H. W. Bush*

He is probably choking on a pretzel or something. I hope nobody tells him that I have won this award while he is eating a pretzel. He has the funniest lines in the film. I am eternally grateful to him.

> —*documentary filmmaker Michael Moore, on President George W. Bush, after winning the top prize at the Cannes Film Festival for* Fahrenheit 9/11

Wretched half-bright swine.
> —*Hunter S. Thompson, on President George W. Bush*

Florida governor Jeb Bush says he wants to be president. Well that's good, somebody will have to pardon his brother.
> —*David Letterman*

Bush said his brother, Jeb, would make a great president. That's all we need. Big Brother's little brother.
> —*Bill Maher*

Rumor is that President Bush's brother, Florida governor Jeb Bush, may run for president. According to Florida voting machines, he's already won.

—*Jay Leno*

The president said his brother Jeb "would be a great president." I guess we voted for the wrong one then.

—*Jimmy Kimmel, host of ABC's* Jimmy Kimmel Live

Agnostics against Bush—some things we know for sure.

—*bumper sticker*

Condoleezza Rice was on every network morning show today blaming this whole mess on "flawed intelligence." Afterward the president took her into his office and said, "You weren't talking about me were you?"

—Bill Maher, on President George W. Bush and the failure to find weapons of mass destruction in Iraq

The unpleasant sound [George W.] Bush is emitting as he traipses from one conservative gathering to another is a thin, tinny "arf"—the sound of a lapdog.

—George F. Will

Bush reiterated his stand to conservatives opposing his decision on stem-cell research. He said today he believes life begins at conception and ends at execution.

—*Jay Leno*

Did the training wheels fall off?
—*Senator John Kerry after being told by reporters that President George W. Bush took a tumble during a bike ride*

You know, this president invaded a sovereign nation in defiance of the U.N. He is basically a war criminal. Honestly. George W. Bush should be tried at The Hague.

—*comic Rosie O'Donnell*

Poor George. He can't help it—he was born with a silver foot in his mouth.

—*State Treasurer Ann Richards of Texas in a keynote address to the Democratic National Convention in 1988, on Republican presidential nominee George H. W. Bush*

George W. Bush is the greatest tyrant in the world, the greatest terrorist in the world.

—singer Harry Belafonte

President [George W.] Bush made a surprise visit to Iraq today. It lasted five hours. Five hours? That's longer than he stayed at any National Guard meetings.

—Jay Leno

George W. Bush doesn't care about black people.

—rapper Kanye West, going off-script during a Hurricane Katrina relief broadcast

Republicans feel that George W. Bush is a tough, strong guy. They still feel that he is avenging 9/11. I don't think he inspires patriotism. You have to understand that this guy's crazy. He's terrible and he's nuts. I think that Bush is waiting for the end of the world.

—Randi Rhodes, Air America talk-show host

If he uses the "mixed messages" line one more time, I'm going to puke.

—John Green, ABC's executive news producer,
on President George W. Bush

[The] worst president ever.

—veteran White House reporter, Helen Thomas,
on George W. Bush

Bush speaks to the audience as if they're idiots. I think the reason he does that is because that's the way these issues were explained to him.
                    —Vanity Fair *editor Graydon Carter,*
                       on Real Time with Bill Maher

I am more patriotic than this president we have, who I consider a traitor of human and American principles.
                    —*Sean Penn, on George W. Bush*

You know what they say in Texas, Chris: "Bobcat can eat all the chili he wants, doesn't mean he's gonna crap diamonds."
> —*columnist Molly Ivins discussing President George W. Bush on* Hardball with Chris Matthews

There was one embarrassing moment for President Bush. When he heard there were forged documents that had been discovered, he said: "What? You mean they found my diploma from Yale?"
> —*Jay Leno, on George W. Bush*

Since taking office, George W. Bush has held nine press conferences, which is way too many. He should prerecord his four answers and every so often Press Secretary Ari Fleischer could play them for the reporters.

—*satirist Mark Russell*

He' a Boy Scout with a hormone imbalance.

—*author Kevin Phillips, on President George W. Bush*

A phony lightweight who bled the treasury dry.

—*columnist Robert Scheer, on President George W. Bush*

I would like to apologize for referring to George W. Bush as a "deserter." What I meant to say is that George W. Bush is a deserter, an election thief, a drunk driver, a WMD liar, and a functional illiterate.

Michael Moore

Just so you know, we're ashamed the president of the United States is from Texas.

—Dixie Chicks' Natalie Maines, at a London concert

Did you see President George W. Bush land on the aircraft carrier?
President Bush told reporters on the carrier after he landed that the
pilot actually let him fly the plane for a little bit. In a related story,
Dick Cheney said that he once let President Bush run the country for
a few minutes.

—*Conan O'Brien*

The first time I met Bush, two things became clear. One, he didn't
know very much. The other was that he had the confidence to ask
questions that revealed he didn't know very much.

—*Richard Perle, foreign policy adviser,*
on President George W. Bush

George W. Bush did some things you could never get away with at your job. When Bush started his job, there was a budget surplus. Now there's like a $70 trillion deficit. Now just imagine you worked at the Gap. You're closing out your register and it's $70 trillion short. The average person would get in trouble for that. Then he started a war? You're $70 trillion behind on your register, and you start a war with Banana Republic because you know they're selling better tank tops than you. So now you've got employees bleeding all over the khakis. Then you finally take over Banana Republic, and you find out they never made tank tops in the first place.

—*comic Chris Rock*

If ignorance ever goes to $40 a barrel, I want drilling rights on George H. W. Bush's head.

—*radio commentator Jim Hightower in 1988*

Wow, wow, what an honor. To just sit here, at the same table with my hero, George W. Bush, to be this close to the man. I feel like I'm dreaming. Somebody pinch me. You know what, I'm a pretty sound sleeper; that may not be enough. Somebody shoot me in the face.

—The Daily Show's *Stephen Colbert at the 2006 White House correspondents' dinner*

All presidents are in a bubble, but the boy king was so insulated he was in a thermos.

—*Maureen Dowd, on President George W. Bush*

President George W. Bush said immigrants should speak English. He then went to a school and had to address the kids in Spanish. Only fifteen years ago he was a failed oil man and someday he will go down in history as the founder of New Spain.

—comic and writer Argus Hamilton

[George W.] Bush may not have been born stupid, but he has achieved stupidity, and now he wears it as a badge of honor.

—Jacob Weisberg, Slate.com editor

President George W. Bush has been hard at work trying to make it illegal for gay people to get married lately. It's a suspicious move for an ex-male cheerleader, I have to say.

—Jimmy Kimmel

Many people make fun of George W. Bush because they say he's simple, backwoods, or clinically retarded. Hey, I think it's wrong to judge. Besides, we should be proud of our president, especially if he's retarded. What other country can make that claim? And it says something about how efficient and well organized the corporations who actually run this government are. They could let a chimp run the show.

—comic Randy Harken

The last time someone listened to a Bush, folks wandered around the desert for forty years.

—Anonymous

The U.S. Senate passed an amendment to the immigration bill naming the English language to be the national language of the United States. It will not become law. President [George W.] Bush would never sign a bill that could get him impeached.

—*Argus Hamilton*

The only way I can describe it is that, well, the president is like a blind man in a room full of deaf people. There is no discernible connection.

—*Paul O'Neill, former treasury secretary, on President George W. Bush*

IV

ELEPHANTIASIS

THE REPUBLICAN PARTY, originally named the Gallant Old Party (not the Grand Old Party), was founded in the 1850s by antislavery activists and those seeking free land in the West. It soon moved into the White House courtesy of Honest Abe.

So what went wrong along the way with the GOP?

Why does it seem more like the "Greedy Old Party"?

Why are its ranks bloated with talk-show big mouths, stiff-necked conservatives, intrusive moralists, and reactionary fossils? Maybe the answer has something to do with the party symbol—the elephant—that was based on an 1874 drawing by political cartoonist Thomas Nash.

An elephant is big and powerful, but most of all, it's a menace—unless it's got an attentive trainer riding its neck, kicking it into obedience. Despite the popular saying, "an elephant never forgets," any handler will tell you that not only is a pachyderm forgetful, it also resents being reminded about anything.

Of course it hurts, you're getting screwed by an elephant!
                                        —*bumper sticker*

Lincoln was right about not fooling all the people all the time.
But the Republicans haven't given up trying.
                                —*President Lyndon B. Johnson*

As long as the Republicans keep serving up the same worthless ideas,
the American people won't care who's running the GOP.
                                        —*James Carville*

The elephant is the perfect symbol for Republicans: they lead each other around by the tail, and think everyone should work for peanuts.

> —*Democratic Party strategist and consultant Bob Schrum*

I have the feeling about 60 percent of what you say is crap.

> —*David Letterman, speaking to Fox News Channel commentator Bill O'Reilly*

The woman suing Bill O'Reilly for unwanted phone sex is allegedly asking for $60 million in damages. That sounds like a lot, until you figure it works out to about $2.99 a minute.

> —*Tina Fey, Saturday Night Live's "Weekend Update"*

The Republicans would know how to fix your tire, but they wouldn't bother to stop because they'd want to be on time for Ugly Pants Night at the country club.

—humorist Dave Barry

Even in a time of elephantine vanity and greed, one never has to look far to see the campfires of gentle people.

—writer and humorist Garrison Keillor

How did sex come to be thought of as dirty in the first place? God must have been a Republican.

—*Will Durst*

There are so many ways to show your patriotism under this Republican regime. You can wave a flag or you can shut your mouth.

—*Randy Harken*

What does a liberal Republican do? Fight to keep everything
the same?

—*Martin Higgins*

For those of you who don't understand Reaganomics, it's based on the
principle that the rich and the poor will get the same amount of ice.
In Reaganomics, however, the poor get all of theirs in winter.

—*Representative Morris K. Udall*

Q: How does an Eisenhower doll work?
A: You wind it up, and it does nothing for eight years.

—*popular joke*

A good Republican is one who doesn't want anybody to know it.

—*James Carville*

House Republicans proposed a pro-war resolution designed to make antiwar Democrats look soft on terror. It never fails. Whenever President Bush delivers his Tarzan yell, all the elephants in the jungle come running to rescue him.

—*Argus Hamilton*

I never dared to be radical when I was young, for fear I would become conservative when I was old.

—poet Robert Frost

If I talk over people's heads, Ike must talk under their feet.

—Senator Adlai Stevenson, on President Eisenhower

When fascism comes to America, it will be wrapped in the flag, carrying a cross.

—novelist Sinclair Lewis

Because you need me, Springfield. Your guilty conscience may force you to vote Democratic, but deep down inside you secretly long for a cold-hearted Republican to lower taxes, brutalize criminals, and rule you like a king. That's why I did this: to protect you from yourselves. Now if you'll excuse me, I have a city to run.

—*Sideshow Bob*, The Simpsons

Relax, there's no Rush.

—Air America *slogan*

For once Rush can't be accused of not knowing what he's
talking about.
　　—*Jay Leno, on Rush Limbaugh doing commercials for Pizza Hut*

Rush Limbaugh is a big, fat idiot.

　　　　　　　　　　　　　　　　　—*comic Al Franken*

Why all the fuss about Rush Limbaugh losing his hearing in 2001,
when he stopped listening in 1974?

　　　　　　　　　　　　　　　　　—*Martin Higgins*

Newt Gingrich is the most unpopular politician in America. His favorable rating is only four points higher than the Unabomber.
                                                        —*Al Franken*

Once he makes up his mind, he's full of indecision.
        —*Hollywood wit Oscar Levant, on President Eisenhower*

I've heard that the Republicans in the Senate are introducing a bill to rewrite the Constitution on an Etch-A-Sketch.
                                                        —*Randy Harken*

Tom DeLay is a man made of iron and brawn and polysynthetic fake hairpieces.

—Wonkette.com, on the former House majority leader

I'm going to miss him too. Another classy move from a classy guy. The man who stood tall even as his staffers dropped like laundered nickels from an Indian casino slot machine. He's doing it right folks—going out at the top of his game in the middle of a criminal investigation.

—Stephen Colbert, on Tom DeLay

Tom DeLay said Americans treat Christianity like some second-rate superstition. To drive home the issue, Tom DeLay said, "Just because I'm a prick, do I not bleed?"

—*Bill Maher*

House majority leader Tom DeLay says he is innocent of all wrong-doing and is the victim of a plot by the Democrats. Fox News does too; they've been spinning this story so hard they had to give the staff Dramamine today.

—*Jimmy Kimmel*

Yeah, we'll miss the old bastard—he knew how to be a majority leader, dammit. It's about taking the R. J. Reynolds corporate jet to your arraignment and not giving a shit.

—Wonkette.com, on Tom DeLay

Tom DeLay is giving up his seat. Well, actually he's not giving it up. He's selling it to the highest bidder on eBay.

—Jay Leno

Tom DeLay gave his farewell speech to the House of Representatives. A brilliant speech and I believe someday DeLay's final address
to Congress will be mentioned in the same breath as the preamble
to the Constitution, the Declaration of Independence, and the
Gettysburg Address. In fact, I just did it. That someday is today.

—*Stephen Colbert*

At the Pentagon, Secretary of Defense Donald Rumsfeld said that the
decision to pay recruits in gasoline, while unorthodox, was a "slam-
dunk solution" to the Army's nagging shortfalls in enlistment.

—*humorist Andy Borowitz*

Karl Rove, he is very desperate now. He's trying to improve his image. And, this afternoon, earlier today, he was jumping up and down on Oprah's couch.

—*David Letterman*

I thought this was nice—earlier today Martha Stewart showed Karl Rove how to slip off an ankle monitor.

—*Jay Leno*

Suspicion for the leak was immediately cast on White House adviser and longtime Bush confidant, Karl Rove, known as one of the few men in Washington with flesh-colored hair.

—Jon Stewart

As with mosquitoes, horseflies, and most bloodsucking parasites, Kenneth Starr was spawned in stagnant water.

—James Carville, on the U.S. independent prosecutor during the Clinton Administration

Governor Jeb Bush prepared Floridians for Hurricane Alberto. He urged everybody to stock up on bottled water and to get all their important papers in order. When the hurricane passes, the immigration service is going to do a bed check.

—*Argus Hamilton*

Some fellows get credit for being conservative when they are only stupid.

—*humorist Frank Hubbard*

It makes sense for the Republicans to limit our freedoms. Why do the terrorists hate us? They don't hate us, they hate our freedoms. So, you take away our freedoms, and you take away the reasons for terrorists to hate us. It's genius!

—Randy Harken

The Republican National Committee has announced it's changing the emblem of the Republican Party—from an elephant to a condom. The condom accepts inflation, halts production, destroys the next generation, protects a bunch of pricks, and gives you a sense of security while you're actually being screwed.

—Bob Schrum

When Republican speechmakers think they are thinking, they are only rearranging their prejudices.

—*Senator Adlai Stevenson*

He's a morality-issues Christian Right Republican. So he's probably a drug-addicted gambling gay adulterer with illegitimate children.

—*Wonkette.com, on Claude Allen, former White House domestic policy adviser charged with theft from a department store*

I don't like Condoleezza Rice because of her politics. I don't like Condoleezza Rice because she's a murderer. You know, I'm not bound by the rules of a politician or journalist.

—*Aaron McGruder, creator of comic strip* The Boondocks

Why are we still in Iraq? We could end this war tomorrow, it's simple. We build a Wal-Mart, McDonald's, and Krispy Kreme in every village in Iraq. A Starbucks on every corner, and a Hummer dealership in the middle of town. I say it's time we fight evil with evil. How long can you stay angry when you start every day with a hot, frothy latte and freshly glazed Krispy Kreme, driving a Hummer to your job at Wal-Mart. Life is good. It wouldn't take long before they're just as fat and lazy as Americans.

—*Randy Harken*

A broomstick in my closet was missing. I asked someone about it and he said, "Ann Coulter took it." "What did she do with it?" I asked. "She's flying around on it as a witch, looking for more 9/11 widows for a follow-up book called *The Coulter Code*."

—*Art Buchwald, writing from his hospice bed*

It slipped my mind that Coulter had a mother. [She] leaves the impression that she would kill someone to be on TV.

—*columnist Margaret Carlson*

How does a venomous harpy who doesn't even believe the hate that she spews continue to play a part in our national conversation?

—*Gawker.com, on Ann Coulter*

Chris Matthews: Do you find her physically attractive, Tucker?
Tucker Carlson: I'm not going to answer that, because the answer,
I don't want to hurt anybody's feelings. That's not
the point.
Chris Matthews: Well, she doesn't pass the Chris Matthews test.
—Hardball with Chris Matthews *on MSNBC,*
on Ann Coulter

We violate her. There are cigarette burns in some funny places. She's
a pure snake-oil salesman. She doesn't believe a word she says.
—*Sean Penn, on his Ann Coulter plastic doll*

Ann Coulter wants everyone to either love her or consider her an
idiot, but she won't take the pay cut to become president.
—*Argus Hamilton*

I wish we lived in the America of yesteryear that only exists in the minds of us Republicans.

—*Ned Flanders*, The Simpsons

The Bush budget, with all the lies in it and wrapped in a flag, that is flag desecration.

—*James Carville*

I like how if you criticize the [Iraq] war, you don't support the troops. You're the ones sending them over to die, so how is it I don't support them? If we went to an all-child-molester army, I would be their biggest supporter. "Please don't bring the troops home. Stay the course."

—*comic Larry David*

They have conned the American people into thinking there is such a
thing as a pro-life, pro-war, pro-gun, pro-death-penalty Christian.
　　　　　　—*Janeane Garofalo*, Air America *talk-show host,*
　　　　　　　　　　referring to conservative talk radio

George W. Bush is a wartime president, he says proudly. Guess what.
When you are at war, you have failed! When you have gone to a war
of choice and lied about it, you're a double-triple, triple-quadruple
failure! It's called a warlord in other countries. One man's ceiling, I
guess, is another man's floor.

　　　　　　　　　　　　　　　　　　—*Janeane Garofalo*

It seems to be a law of nature that Republicans are more boring than Democrats.

>—*columnist Stewart Alsop*

This administration is soaring. If anything, they are rearranging the deck chairs on the *Hindenburg*.

>—*Stephen Colbert at the White House*
>*Correspondents Dinner, 2006*

His writing is rumble and bumble, flap and doodle, balder and dash.

>—*H. L. Mencken, on President Warren Harding*

Making fun of born-again Christians is like hunting dairy cows with a high-powered rifle and scope.

—humorist P. J. O'Rourke

The people are wise—wiser than the Republicans think.

—Senator Adlai Stevenson

The Republican Party either corrupts its liberals or it expels them.

—President Harry S. Truman

No children have ever meddled with the Republican Party and lived to tell about it.

—*Sideshow Bob,* The Simpsons

The incredible dullness wreaked upon the American landscape in Eisenhower's eight years has been a triumph of the corporation. A tasteless, sexless, odorless sanctity in architecture, manners, modes, styles has been the result.

—*author Norman Mailer, 1963*

When you are right you cannot be too radical; when you are wrong, you cannot be too conservative.

—*Dr. Martin Luther King Jr.*

The Democratic Party at its worst is better than the Republican Party at its best.

—*President Lyndon B. Johnson*

You never had to ask his score. Just count his casualties.

—*Bob Hope, on Vice President Spiro Agnew's golf game*

When Agnew yelled "Fore!", you never knew whether he was telling someone to get out of the way or if he was predicting how many spectators he would hit with a shot.

—*Bob Hope*

The function of liberal Republicans is to shoot the wounded after battle.

—*Senator Eugene McCarthy*

If life were fair, Dan Quayle would be making a living asking,
"Do you want fries with that?"
                    —*comedian John Cleese, on the former vice president*

Republicans sleep in twin beds—some even in separate rooms.
                                    —*writer and actor Will Stanton*

In a very Christian way, as far as I'm concerned, he can go to hell.
                    —*President Jimmy Carter, on Reverend Jerry Falwell*

Laffer Curve? That's Big Business laughing all the way to the bank.

—*David Feldman*

Conservatism is the worship of dead revolutions.

—*author Clinton Rossiter*

In the United States I have always believed that there was a big difference between conservative and stupid. Boy, is it getting harder to prove that one by the minute.

—*blogger Rick Mercer*

The radical right is so homophobic that they're blaming global warming on the AIDS quilt.

—*Dennis Miller*

The 1928 Republican Convention opened with a prayer. If the Lord can see his way clear to bless the Republican Party the way it's been carrying on, then the rest of us ought to get it without even asking.

—*humorist Will Rogers*

Jim Bakker spells his name with two *k*'s because three would be too obvious.

—*Bill Maher, on the television evangelist and convicted felon*

Most thinking people agree with the need for mandatory school prayer. What rankles them is the lack of algebra instruction in church.

—*comic William Weil*

Today, a liberal Republican is one who thinks a condemned man getting death by injection should be laid out on a comfy mattress.

—*Dennis Miller*

To be a Republican is to deny you are a Republican.

—*James Carville*

Vice President Dick Cheney, while hunting wild geese in the Rose Garden, accidentally shot President Bush twice, once in the heart and once in the head. "I didn't really shoot the president twice," said Cheney. "The second time I shot him, I was president."

—*comic Steve Martin*

The truth is, I'm terrified to be here. Not because you're such a tough audience, but because they're serving drinks and I'm standing about thirty yards from the vice president.

—*Senator Barack Obama, at the 2006 Gridiron Press Dinner*

Here now a list of requirements for Dick Cheney's "downtime suite":
He wants bottled water. He wants decaffeinated coffee. He wants
an ice bucket. He wants ammo. Cheney wants bottled water, decaffeinated coffee. He wants his lights on. He wants the temperature
at 68 degrees, the TVs must be tuned to Fox News. I was thinking,
"My God, I wish they would have put this much preparation into the
Iraqi war."

—*David Letterman, on the vice president*

The Democrats and Republicans are equally corrupt—it's only in the
amount where the Republicans excel.

—*Will Rogers*

You have to have been a Republican to know how good it is to be a Democrat.

—*Jacqueline Kennedy Onassis*

I'm working on a song about Alberto Gonzales, but I can't find a rhyme for thumbscrews.

—*satirist Mark Russell, on the attorney general*

Jessica Simpson turned down an invitation to meet President [George W.] Bush at a fund-raiser. Yeah, Bush said he invited Simpson because he likes being around people who challenge him.

—*Conan O'Brien*

They keep talking about drafting a constitution for Iraq. Why don't we just give them ours? It was written by a lot of really smart guys, it's worked for over two hundred years, and we're not using it anymore.

—*comic George Carlin*

Most of us have learned to simply accept the fact that Rupert Murdoch's News Corp. exists in the world, just as we've come to accept that there are terrorists among us, as well as people who scam grandmothers out of their savings.

—*Keith Olbermann, host of MSNBC's*
Countdown with Keith Olbermann

There isn't any finer folks living than a Republican that votes the Democratic ticket.

—*Will Rogers*

President Bush made fun of a White House reporter for wearing sunglasses, not knowing the guy was blind. He should have known. The only reporters who can still get White House press credentials are either blind, deaf, or with Fox News.

—*Argus Hamilton*

A nervous, shifty, sweaty, petulant, mental adolescent.
 —writer Camille Paglia, on former representative Newt Gingrich

A conservative is a man who just thinks and sits, mostly sits.
        —President Woodrow Wilson

Republicans can party almost as much as porn stars. I was getting propositions to have threesomes with wives or mistresses, I was offered money from oil tycoons.
 —porn star Mary Carey, California recall ballot gubernatorial candidate, on attending a Republican Party fund-raiser

I'm especially looking forward to meeting Karl Rove. Smart men like him are so sexy. I know that he's against gay marriage, but I think I can convince him that a little girl-on-girl action now and then isn't so bad!

> —*Mary Carey, on being invited to dine*
> *with President George W. Bush*

If George Bush had selected the court in '54, Clarence Thomas would have never got to law school.

> —*Michael Moore, on the Supreme Court justice*

My view is that Fox News is a propaganda outlet for the Republican Party and I don't comment on Fox News.

> —*Democratic National Committee Chairman Howard Dean*

A seething nest of proto-fascist impulses.

—*Camille Paglia, on Senator John McCain*

When Kissinger can get the Nobel Peace Prize, what is there left for satire?

—*satirist Tom Lehrer*

The Christian Right is neither.

—*singer Moby*

The Republicans don't care about the working poor—they don't know any.

—*James Carville*

I like getting lectures on values and hard work from Dan Quayle, who recently charged the taxpayers $27,000 for a golf weekend.
—*Molly Ivins, on the former vice president*

It's too bad Moses is so wrong on this one.
—*Representative Nita Lowey on Charlton Heston's opposition to gun control*

Golf had long symbolized the Eisenhower years—played by soft, boring men with ample waistlines who went round rich men's country-club courses in the company of wealthy businessmen and were tended by white-haired, dutiful Negroes.

—*author David Halberstam*

Whenever I play with him, I usually try to make it a foursome—the president, myself, a paramedic, and a faith healer.

—*Bob Hope, on President Gerald Ford's erratic golf game*

How come you're so wrong, my sweet neo-con? / You call yourself a Christian, I call you a hypocrite. / You call yourself a patriot. Well, I think you're full of shit!
　　　—Mick Jagger singing a refrain from "Sweet Neo Con," a track
　　　　　　　　from A Bigger Bang, *the Rolling Stones latest CD*

This is the Law and Order and Terror government. It promised protection—or at least amelioration—against all threats: conventional, radiological, or biological. It has just proved that it cannot save its citizens from a biological weapon called standing water.
　　　　　　　—Keith Olbermann, on New Orleans's
　　　　　　　flooding following Hurricane Katrina

Once he makes up his mind, he's full of indecision.
>   —*Oscar Levant, on President Eisenhower*

Full Dinner Jacket.
>   —*Jay Leno, speculating on a name for a movie biography*
>   *of Dan Quayle, who did not serve in Vietnam*

Danny, the cabin boy for the captain of the Titanic.
>   —*former New York governor Mario Cuomo,*
>   *during a feud with Dan Quayle*

Dressing is a matter of taste, and I've met very few Republicans with good taste.

—*former San Francisco mayor Willie Brown*

I like that about the Republicans; the evidence does not faze them, they are not bothered at all by the facts.

—*President Bill Clinton*

He's a nice guy, but he played too much football with his helmet off.

—*President Lyndon B. Johnson, on President Gerald Ford*

Humpty-Dumpty.

—*President Franklin Delano Roosevelt,*
on his White House predecessor Herbert Hoover

Brains, you know, are suspect in the Republican Party.

—*columnist Walter Lippman*

I have long enjoyed the friendship and companionship of Republicans because I am by instinct a teacher, and I would like to teach them something.

—*President Woodrow Wilson*

I have been thinking that I would make a proposition to my Republican friends . . . that if they will stop telling lies about the Democrats, we will stop telling the truth about them.

—*Senator Adlai Stevenson*

When I started in this business, everybody said the Democrats were the better communicators because they sounded like social workers, and Republicans were awful because they sounded like morticians. In some cases they actually dressed like morticians.

—*pollster Frank Luntz*

Once you leave the womb, conservatives don't care about you until
you reach military age. Then you're just what they're looking for.

—*George Carlin*

I am really enjoying the new Martin Luther King Jr. stamp—
just think about all those white bigots, licking the backside of a
black man.

—*comic Dick Gregory*

A compassionate conservative is someone who electrocutes juveniles
but lets them have a last "make a wish."

—*Garrison Keillor*

This blizzard of mind-warping war propaganda out of Washington is building up steam. Monday is Anthrax, Tuesday is Bankruptcy, Friday is Child-Rape, Thursday is Bomb-scares, etc., etc., etc. . . . If we believed all the brutal, frat-boy threats coming out of the White House, we would be dead before Sunday. It is pure and savage terrorism reminiscent of Nazi Germany.

—*Hunter S. Thompson*

When a nation's young men are conservative, its funeral bell is already rung.

—*theologian and author Henry Ward Beecher*

Republicans in the House of Representatives forced everyone to spend an entire day discussing a nonbinding resolution praising the troops and labeling Iraq part of the War on Terror. Later they will debate a resolution declaring kittens "adorable."

—Jon Stewart

1/20/09—End of an Error

—bumper sticker

Republicans in the Senate have announced they are moving on from gay marriage to a constitutional amendment to ban flag burning. We would join the only three other countries who have banned flag burning: China, Cuba, and Iran. We can stand with our brothers on this issue.

—*Jay Leno*

They say that Attorney General John Ashcroft may be stepping down. Apparently he wants to spend more time spying on his family.

—*David Letterman*

Why does listening to John Ashcroft make me feel like the world has already ended? If we're going to be warned about terrorism, can't it be by someone who actually makes us want to live?

—Jon Stewart, on the former attorney general's announcement that America's terror-alert level had been raised from yellow to orange

Kind of a sad study out today that single women over the age of thirty-five are more likely to be shot by the vice president than to find a husband.

—Jimmy Kimmel, on Dick Cheney

I guess we're all excited that President Bush announced his nomina-
tion to the Supreme Court—John Roberts. Bush searched far and
wide before he made the risky choice of a white guy in his fifties.

—*David Letterman*

William Bennett, the man they call the moral voice of America, lost
almost $8 million playing slot machines. And here is the amazing
part: He still has a better economic plan than President Bush.

—*Jay Leno*

New York Mayor Rudy Giuliani is once again expressing outrage at an art exhibit, this time at a painting in which Jesus is depicted as a naked woman. Said the mayor, "This trash is not the sort of thing that I want to look at when I go to the museum with my mistress."

—*Tina Fey*, Saturday Night Live's *"Weekend Update"*

Compared with the BBC's studied neutrality, Fox comes across as a kind of *Gong Show* of propaganda.

—*columnist Russ Baker*

Liberals feel unworthy of their possessions. Conservatives feel they deserve everything they've stolen.

—*Mort Sahl*

All conservatives are such from personal defects. They have been effeminated by position or nature, born halt and blind, through luxury of their parents, and can only, like invalids, act on the defensive.

—author and philosopher Ralph Waldo Emerson

A conservative is someone who makes no changes and consults his grandmother when in doubt.

—President Woodrow Wilson

Not Eavesdropping, Freedom Listening

—bumper sticker

I've left specific instructions that I do not want to be brought back during a Republican administration.

*—Pyschologist and LSD advocate Timothy Leary,
on being kept cryogenically frozen*

Republicans are against abortion until their daughters need one.

—educator Gracie McGarvie

I don't want to see the Republican Party ride to political victory on the Four Horsemen of Calumny—Fear, Ignorance, Bigotry, and Smear.

—Senator Margaret Chase Smith

It is important that the United States remain a two-party system. I'm a fellow who likes small parties, and the Republican Party can't be too small to suit me.

—*President Lyndon B. Johnson*

There are few things more amusing in the world of politics than watching moderate Republicans charging to the right in pursuit of greater glory.

—*former New York governor Mario Cuomo*

The Republicans have a new healthcare proposal: Just say no
to illness!

—*Mark Russell*

The GOP being the party of white Christians.

—*Howard Dean*

How can they tell?

—*writer Dorothy Parker, on hearing of
President Calvin Coolidge's death*

If guns are outlawed, how will conservatives win any arguments?

—*Anonymous*

The GOP: A rising tide lifts all yachts.

—*Anonymous*

GOP – Greed Over Patriotism.

—*bumper sticker*

The Secret Service arrested a man for acting strangely around Dick Cheney in Vail. Agents said the man was detained because he wasn't acting like other folks. He told the vice president he really supports what he is doing in Iraq.

—*Argus Hamilton*

Conservatives are *Reichwing*.

—*graffiti*

We are losing the democracy that we're trying to sell in the Mideast and everywhere else right here in our own nation.

—*Rosie O'Donnell*

At this point, why don't we just hand Halliburton the keys to the U.S. Treasury and tell them to turn off the lights when they are done.

—*Senator Frank Lautenberg*

⌒

Condi Rice received six standing ovations at the Southern Baptist Convention annual meeting. They worship the same God. In the closing ceremony, they all bowed their heads, held hands, and vowed to follow Jesus into Iran.

—*Argus Hamilton, on the Secretary of State*

⌒

This week, Georgia's board of education approved a plan that allows teachers to keep using the word "evolution" when teaching biology. Though, as a compromise, dinosaurs are now called "Jesus Horses."

—*Jimmy Fallon, Saturday Night Live's "Weekend Update"*

⌒

The Religious Right scares the hell out of me.

—*Senator Barry Goldwater*

How does the Religious Right have all this time and energy to protest gay marriage? Shouldn't they be preparing to battle ten-horned demons, lions with wings, and the Antichrist?

—*Martin Higgins*

South Dakota governor Mike Rounds on Monday signed legislation banning almost all abortions in the state. As a result, South Dakota is changing its motto from "Under God, the People Rule" to "You should have thought of that before prom."

—*Tina Fey*, Saturday Night Live's "*Weekend Update*"

In an effort to regain the ethical high ground in Washington, Republican Party leaders announced a series of lobbying reforms. This is kind of like foxes calling for a new collection of locks to be placed on the henhouse. Which they get to install.

—Will Durst

He'll sit up there and he'll say, "Do this! Do that!" and nothing will happen. Poor Ike—it won't be a bit like the army.

—President Harry S. Truman, on his successor,
Dwight Eisenhower

There are some Republicans I would trust with anything—anything, that is, except public office.

—Senator Adlai Stevenson

A conservative is a man who wants the rules changed so that no one can make a pile the way he did.

—*humorist Gregory Nunn*

Republicans no longer worship at the shrine of a balanced budget.

—*former Representative Jack Kemp and Republican Party vice presidential nominee in 1996*

Do you know what a conservative is? That's a liberal who got mugged the night before.

—*former Philadelphia police chief and mayor Frank Rizzo*

The Republican Party makes even its young men seem old; the Democratic Party makes even its old men seem young.

Senator Adlai Stevenson

Antichoice protesters call for adoption rather than abortion. It's their version of "Get a life!"

Martin Higgins

You can't make the Republican Party pure by more contributions, because contributions are what got it where it is today.

—Will Rogers

Reaganomics, that makes sense to me. It means if you don't have enough money, it's because poor people are hoarding it.

—*comic and actor Kevin Rooney*

A conservative is a man with two perfectly good legs who, however, has never learned how to walk forward.

—*President Franklin Delano Roosevelt in a 1939 radio address*

It seems to be a law of nature that Republicans are more boring than Democrats.

—*columnist Stewart Alsop*

Former Senator Bob Dole revealed he is one of the test subjects for Viagra. He said on Larry King, "I wish I had bought stock in it." Only a Republican would think the best part of Viagra is the fact that you could make money off of it.

—*Jay Leno*

White House press secretary Scott McClellan lost his job to Fox News radio host Tony Snow. So far, the Bush Administration seems pleased with the Snow job.

—*Martin Higgins*

Rumsfeld is treated as an eccentric old uncle who pops off and is ignored.

> —*Maureen Dowd, quoting a Bush administration official on the secretary of defense*

The Republicans stroke platitudes until they purr like epigrams.

> —*Senator Adlai Stevenson*

V

ELECTION CYCLE

ELECTION CAMPAIGNS seem to have more in common with the rinse, wash, and spin cycles of laundromats than with voters reluctantly heading to the polls every two or four years. After election day, guess who is left out to dry. We are.

Candidates get their personal dirty laundry examined. As teams of consultants and media handlers use spot remover to remove the mud that's been slung, they also craft the spin.

How often do voters hear "New and Improved!" from candidates seeking public office? At least, it's easy to now separate the blues from the reds.

I didn't vote for you, but you have a nice suit on.
—*Don Meredith, upon meeting Nixon's running mate Spiro Agnew during ABC's* Monday Night Football

I figured out Karl Rove's political strategy—make gas so expensive, no Democrats can afford to go to the polls.
—*Senator John Kerry*

The day Dick Cheney is going to run for president, I'll kill myself. All we need is one more liar.
—*Helen Thomas*

What makes him think a middle-aged actor, who's played with a chimp, could have a future in politics?

> —*Ronald Reagan, on Clint Eastwood's*
> *bid to become mayor of Carmel*

Why do Republicans fear debate? For the same reason baloney fears the slicer.

> —*Democratic Party vice presidential*
> *nominee Senator Lloyd Bentsen*

The Republicans are the party that says government doesn't work and then they get elected and prove it.

> —*P. J. O'Rourke*

A lot of people were surprised that Ford picked Nelson Rockefeller to run with him; after all, Rocky had tried to get the job of president three times himself. That's like asking Morris the Cat to watch your tuna salad.

—Bob Hope

Every Republican candidate for president since 1936 has been nominated by the Chase National Bank.

—Senator Robert A. Taft

Voters quickly forget what a man says.

—Richard Nixon

It's Robert Dole's misfortune that when he does smile, he looks like he's just evicted a widow.

columnist Mike Royko, on the Republican Party
vice presidential nominee

Dole's married to the head of the American Red Cross, so he can get fresh blood whenever he wants.

—comic and writer Harry Shearer

In a recent fire Bob Dole's library burned down. Both books were lost. And he hadn't even finished coloring one of them.

—Representative Jack Kemp, during the 1996
Republican presidential primary

I had a truly horrible dream last night. Arnold Schwarzenegger, Mike Tyson, and I were on our way to a TV studio for a debate about his longtime working friendship with the powerful Bush family from Texas and how it might affect the next Bush presidency when The Terminator seizes power in Sacramento and tries to hand over the state's fifty-four electoral votes by election day in 2004. That is the basic plan behind Schwarzenegger running. He doesn't want to be governor, he just wants the electoral votes to go to Bush this time.

—*Hunter S. Thompson*

I feel sorry for Nixon, because he does not know who he is, and at each stop he has to decide which Nixon he is at the moment, which must be very exhausting.

—*John F. Kennedy, during the 1960 presidential campaign*

Jackie Biskupski is running for a seat in the Utah Legislature, and she's attracting a lot of attention because she's a lesbian. Her Republican opponent, Dan Alderson, is a staunch Mormon, and is running a negative ad campaign calling her lifestyle abnormal and deviant. His six wives agree.

—*Rick Mercer*

It was hard to listen to Goldwater and realize that a man could be half Jewish and yet sometimes appear twice as dense as the normal Gentile.

—*I. F. Stone, on the Republican Party presidential nominee in 1964*

If Karl Rove is watching today, Karl, I want you to hear me loud
and clear: I am going to provide tax cuts to ease the burdens for 31
million American families—and lift hundreds of thousands of children
out of poverty—by raising the taxes on 0.1 percent of families—those
who make more than $1,000,000 a year. You don't have to read my
lips, I'm saying it. And if that makes me an "old-style" Democrat, then
I accept that label with pride, and I dare you to come after me for it.

—*General Wesley Clark, during the* 2004
Democratic presidential primaries

It is true that Mr. Lincoln signed the Emancipation Proclamation,
after which there was a commitment to give forty acres and a mule.
That's where the argument, to this day, of reparations starts. We
never got the forty acres. We went all the way to Herbert Hoover,
and we never got the forty acres. We didn't get the mule.
So we decided we'd ride this donkey as far as it would take us.

—*Reverend Al Sharpton speaking at the*
2004 *Democratic National Convention*

The situation in Ohio would give aspirin a headache.
—*CBS anchorperson Dan Rather, on voting snafus in the 2004*
presidential election

Being lectured by the president on fiscal responsibility is a little bit
like Tony Soprano talking to me about law and order in this country.
—*Democratic Party presidential nominee Senator John Kerry,*
speaking after a televised debate with President Bush in 2004

I wanted to have John Edwards stand. Dick Cheney wanted to
sit. We compromised and now George Bush is gonna sit on Dick
Cheney's lap.
—*Senator John Kerry, on discussing negotiations over*
the vice presidential debate in 2004

The big hang-up was George Bush wanted to get lifelines, so he could call somebody.

—*Senator John Kerry, on negotiations over the presidential debates, during an appearance on* Live with Regis and Kelly

⌒

With a paltry legislative record, and receiving campaign contributions from a contractor embroiled in the Duke Cunningham scandal, Katherine Harris is clearly banking her Senate campaign on two things: her spectacular breasts.

—The Daily Show *correspondent Jason Jones on the 2006 Florida Senate race*

⌒

I'd call it a new version of voodoo economics, but I'm afraid that would give witch doctors a bad name.

—Democratic Party vice presidential nominee
Geraldine A. Ferraro, on the Republican Party platform in 1984

I served with Jack Kennedy. I knew Jack Kennedy. Jack Kennedy was a friend of mine. Senator, you're no Jack Kennedy.

—Democratic Party vice presidential nominee Lloyd Bentsen,
speaking directly to Dan Quayle during their debate in 1998

An empty suit that goes to funerals and plays golf.
                    —Independent Party presidential nominee Ross Perot,
                                    on Dan Quayle in 1992

Dan Quayle is more stupid than Ronald Reagan put together.
                                    —comic Matt Groening

If elected, I will win.
                    —Pat Paulsen, satirist and serial presidential candidate

Why am I running for president? Well, my wife, Cindy, says it is because I sustained several severe blows to the head in prison camp.
—Senator John McCain in 2001

President [George W.] Bush appeared with Arnold Schwarzenegger at a huge campaign event. Only in California can a governor who speaks German and a president who can barely speak English try to make themselves clear to an audience that's primarily Spanish.
—Jay Leno

VI

BLOOPERS,
GAFFES,
AND

FOOT-IN-
THE-MOUTH

ALMOST EVERY POLITICIAN LOVES TO TALK AND TALK. The presence of reporters and television cameras often triggers a Pavlovian response that launches an elected official into making a speech. It doesn't even matter if the words are his own—and in all likelihood, they probably aren't.

Luckily for us, Republicans say the strangest things. Whether it's a mangled metaphor or slip of the tongue, these unguarded moments give us a true peek inside the GOP mind.

These gaffes can sometimes be forgotten, leaving behind little lasting damage. But other times, they can sink a political career. Unshaped by speechwriters and untested by focus groups, these unrehearsed sound bites reveal the real person hiding behind the public mask.

You work three jobs? Uniquely American, isn't it? I mean, that is fantastic that you're doing that.

> —*President Bush, speaking to a divorced mother of three in Omaha, Nebraska, in 2005*

I've noticed that everyone who is for abortion has already been born.

> —*President Ronald Reagan*

President Washington, President Lincoln, President Wilson, President Roosevelt have all authorized electronic surveillance on a far broader scale.

> —*Attorney General Alberto Gonzales, testifying before Congress in 2006*

Why should we hear about body bags and deaths? Oh, I mean, it's not relevant. So why should I waste my beautiful mind on something like that?
—former first lady Barbara Bush, speaking about the Iraq War, on Good Morning America, *March 17, 2003*

Considering the dire circumstances that we have in New Orleans, virtually a city that has been destroyed, things are going relatively well.
—former FEMA director Michael Brown, talking to reporters after Hurricane Katrina

I can only speak to myself.
—President George W. Bush

What I'm hearing, which is sort of scary, is that they all want to stay in Texas. Everybody is so overwhelmed by the hospitality. And so many of the people in the arena here, you know, were underprivileged anyway so this (chuckle)—this is working very well for them.

> —*former first lady Barbara Bush, on Hurricane Katrina evacuees at the Houston Astrodome*

Now tell me the truth boys, is this kind of fun?

> —*then House majority leader Tom DeLay, speaking to three young Katrina evacuees at the Astrodome*

I do know that it's true that if you wanted to reduce crime, you could, if that were your sole purpose, you could abort every black baby in this country, and your crime rate would go down.

> —*Bill Bennett, former secretary of education*
> *and radio talk-show host*

My fellow Americans, I'm pleased to tell you today that I've signed legislation that will outlaw Russia forever. We begin bombing in five minutes.

> —*President Ronald Reagan, during a White House*
> *radio broadcast sound check into an open mike*

We know there are known knowns: there are things we know we know. We also know there are known unknowns: that is to say we know there are things we know we don't know. But there are also unknown unknowns—the ones we don't know we don't know.

—*Secretary of Defense Donald Rumsfeld in* 2002,
talking to reporters about Iraq

Our enemies are innovative and resourceful, and so are we. They never stop thinking about new ways to harm our country and our people, and neither do we.

—*President George W. Bush*

Sure, it's going to kill a lot of people, but they may be dying of something else anyway.

—*Othal Brand, member of a Texas pesticide review board, on chlordane*

For seven and a half years I've worked alongside President Reagan. We've had triumphs. Made some mistakes. We've had some sex . . . uh . . . setbacks.

—*Vice President George H. W. Bush*

They're all making love lying up against the pipeline and you got thousands of caribou up there.

—*President George H. W. Bush, on wildlife and the Alaskan pipeline*

It's no exaggeration to say the undecideds could go one way
or another.

—President George H. W. Bush

I'm the decider and I decide what's best. And what's best is for Don
Rumsfeld to remain.

*—President George W. Bush, responding to Iraq war
critics demanding he fire the secretary of defense
for mishandling the Iraq war*

When a great many people are unable to find work,
unemployment results.

*—former President Calvin Coolidge,
on the Great Depression*

If Lincoln was alive today, he'd roll over in his grave.
—President Gerald Ford

Things are more like they are now than they have ever been.
—President Gerald Ford

[Go] f--k yourself.
—Vice President Dick Cheney, speaking to Senator Patrick Leahy

It is unknowable how long that conflict will last. It could last six days, six weeks. I doubt six months.

> —*Secretary of Defense Donald Rumsfeld,*
> *on the Iraq War, February 2003*

You cannot be president of the United States if you don't have faith. Remember Lincoln, going to his knees in times of trial and the Civil War and all that stuff. You can't be. And we are blessed. So don't feel sorry for—don't cry for me, Argentina. Message: I care.

—*President George H. W. Bush, speaking to employees of an insurance company during the 1992 New Hampshire Republican primary*

When the president does it, that means it's not illegal.

> —*President Richard M. Nixon*

If we don't succeed, we run the risk of failure.

—*Vice President Dan Quayle*

You are right phonetically, but what else?

—*Vice President Dan Quayle telling a schoolboy that he misspelled potato because Quayle thought it had an e at the end*

Now, like, I'm president. It would be pretty hard for some drug guy to come into the White House and start offering it up, you know? I bet if they did, I hope I would say, "Hey, get lost. We don't want any of that."

—*President George H.W. Bush, speaking to a group of students about drug abuse*

The Internet is a gateway to get on the Net.
        —*Republican Party presidential nominee Bob Dole in 1996*

Too many good docs are getting out of the business. Too many OB-GYNs aren't able to practice their love with women all across this country.
        —*President George W. Bush*

You can fool some of the people all the time, and those are the ones you want to concentrate on.
        —*President George W. Bush*

It's been a fabulous year for Laura and me.
> —*President George W. Bush, on December 2001,*
> *three months after the World Trade Center attacks*

Fool me once, shame on—shame on you. Fool me—you can't get fooled again.
> —*President George W. Bush*

It's a heck of a place to bring your family.
> —*President George W. Bush, on New Orleans*
> *after Hurricane Katrina*

You took an oath to defend our flag and our freedom, and you kept that oath underseas and under fire.

—President George W. Bush, in a 2006 speech to Veterans of Foreign Wars

As you can possibly see, I have an injury myself—not here at the hospital, but in combat with a cedar. I eventually won. The cedar gave me a little scratch. As a matter of fact, the colonel asked if I needed first aid when she first saw me. I was able to avoid any major surgical operations here, but thanks for your compassion.

—President George W. Bush, after visiting with wounded Iraq War veterans at the Amputee Care Center in San Antonio

Wow! Brazil is big.
    —President George W. Bush, after being shown a map of Brazil
        by Brazilian president Luiz Inacio Lula da Silva

I think it's important to bring somebody from outside the system,
the judicial system, somebody that hasn't been on the bench and,
therefore, there's not a lot of opinions for people to look at.
                    —George W. Bush, on the nomination
                    of Harriet Miers to the Supreme Court

It's totally wiped out. It's devastating, it's got to be doubly devastating on the ground.

—*President George W. Bush, speaking to his aides while surveying Hurricane Katrina flood damage from Air Force One*

I'm looking forward to a good night's sleep on the soil of a friend.

—*President George W. Bush, on visiting Denmark*

The other thing, it turns out, in this job you've got a lot on your plate on a regular basis, you don't have much time to sit around and wander, lonely, in the Oval Office, kind of asking different portraits, how do you think my standing will be?

> —*President George W. Bush pondering how history may view him at a White House press conference*

This notion that the United States is getting ready to attack Iran is simply ridiculous. And having said that, all options are on the table.

> —*President George W. Bush in 2005*

There's Adam Clymer, major-league asshole from the *New York Times*.
—Presidential nominee George W. Bush, in 2000,
speaking to running mate Dick Cheney on the campaign trail

Who could have possibly envisioned an erection—an election in Iraq
at this point in history?

—President George W. Bush

I hope I stand for anti-bigotry, anti-Semitism, anti-racism. This is what drives me.

—President George H. W. Bush in 1988

He didn't say that. He was reading what was given to him in a speech.

—Richard Darman, former director of Office of Management and Budget on explaining why President George W. Bush wasn't following up on his campaign pledge that there would be no loss of wetlands

So many minority youths had volunteered . . . that there was
literally no room for patriotic folks like myself.

> —*former Representative Tom DeLay, explaining at the 1988
> GOP convention why he and vice presidential nominee
> Dan Quayle did not fight in the Vietnam War*

We're no longer a superpower. We're a super-duper power.

> —*Tom DeLay*

Nothing is more important in the face of a war than cutting taxes.

> —*Tom DeLay*

Guns have little or nothing to do with juvenile violence. The causes of youth violence are working parents who put their kids into day-care, the teaching of evolution in the schools, and working mothers who take birth-control pills.

> —*Tom DeLay, on causes of the Columbine High School massacre, 1999*

I couldn't get a job with CIA today. I am not qualified.

> —*former CIA director Porter Goss, in an interview that was conducted while he was still in Congress*

Republicans understand the importance of bondage between a
mother and child.

—*Vice President Dan Quayle*

One word sums up probably the responsibility of any vice president,
and that one word is "to be prepared."

—*Vice President Dan Quayle*

The Holocaust was an obscene period in our nation's history. I mean
in this century's history. But we all lived in this century. I didn't live in
this century.

—*Vice President Dan Quayle*

I have made good judgments in the past. I have made good judgments in the future.

> —*Vice President Dan Quayle*

I love California, I practically grew up in Phoenix.

> —*Vice President Dan Quayle*

It isn't pollution that's harming the environment. It's the impurities in our air and water that are doing it.

> —*Vice President Dan Quayle*

I stand by all the misstatements that I've made.

—*Vice President Dan Quayle*

What a waste it is to lose one's mind—or not to have a mind.

—*Vice President Dan Quayle, addressing
the United Negro College Fund*

As I was telling my husb—

—*Secretary of State Condoleezza Rice, speaking about
George W. Bush, before she corrected herself
at a private dinner party.*

All of a sudden, we see riots, we see protests, we see people clashing. The next thing we know, there is injured or there is dead people. We don't want to get to that extent.
>   —*California governor Arnold Schwarzenegger,*
>   *speaking about the dangers posed by gay marriage*

Get some devastation in the back.
>   —*Senate majority leader Bill Frist, to a staff assistant,*
>   *while posing for a photographer during his visit*
>   *to tsunami-ravaged Sri Lanka*

We know where they are. They're in the area around Tikrit and Baghdad and east, west, south, and north somewhat."

> —*Secretary of Defense Donald Rumsfeld,*
> *on Iraq's weapons of mass destruction*

I am not going to give you a number for it because it's not my business to do intelligent work.

> —*Secretary of Defense Donald Rumsfeld, asked to estimate the*
> *number of Iraqi insurgents while testifying before Congress*

The implication that there was something wrong with the war plan is amusing.

> —*Secretary of Defense Donald Rumsfeld,*
> *responding to Iraq War critics*

I don't do quagmires.

—Secretary of Defense Donald Rumsfeld

I think they're in the last throes, if you will, of the insurgency.

—Vice President Dick Cheney, on the Iraq insurgency in 2005

VII

POLITICAL
BONE PILE

HERE'S A USEFUL COLLECTION of all-purpose one-liners and observations that resist easy categorization. Some of these quotes are newly minted, while others date back to earlier periods in American history. You'll find that there's still some tasty meat on these bones.

Everything is changing. People are taking their comedians seriously and the politicians as a joke.

—*Will Rogers*

If you want a friend in Washington, get a dog.

—*President Harry S. Truman*

I don't make jokes. I just watch the government and report the facts.

—*Will Rogers*

Politics is the art of looking for trouble, finding it everywhere, diagnosing it incorrectly, and applying the wrong remedies.

—*Groucho Marx*

Don't follow leaders, watch your parkin' meters.

—*musician Bob Dylan*

Those who make peaceful revolution impossible will make violent revolution inevitable.

—*President John F. Kennedy*

Presidency, n. The greased pig in the field game of American politics.

—*Ambrose Bierce in* The Devil's Dictionary

There are two things you need for success in politics. Money . . . and I can't think of the other.

—Senator Mark Hannah

Giving money and power to government is like giving whiskey and car keys to teenage boys.

—P. J. O'Rourke

Today's political campaigns function as collection agencies for broadcasters. You simply transfer money from contributors to television stations.

—*Senator Bill Bradley, in* 2000

Washington is a city of southern efficiency and northern charm.

—*President John F. Kennedy*

Everyone is entitled to his own opinion, but not his own facts.

—*Senator Daniel Patrick Moynihan*

A politician is an animal which can sit on a fence and yet keep both ears to the ground.

—*H. L. Mencken*

Politics is the entertainment industry for ugly people.

—*poet Mark Turpin*

It is the first responsibility of every citizen to question authority.

—*Benjamin Franklin*

Bipartisan usually means that a larger-than-usual deception is being carried out.

—George Carlin

If voting changed anything, they'd make it illegal.

—activist Emma Goldman

An honest politician is one who, when he is bought, will stay bought.

—Simon Cameron, Lincoln's first secretary of war

One of the key problems today is that politics is such a disgrace, good people don't go into government.

—*real estate developer Donald Trump*

Every government is run by liars, and nothing they say should be believed.

—*I. F. Stone*

If you attack the establishment long enough and hard enough, they will make you a member of it.

—*Art Buchwald*

A politician's words reveal less about what he thinks about his subject than what he thinks about his audience.

—*columnist George F. Will*

Being elected to Congress is regarded as being sent on a looting raid for one's friends.

—*George F. Will*

A palm-pounding pack of preening pols.
—former White House speechwriter and columnist
William L. Safire, on Congress

The military don't start wars. Politicians start wars.
—General William Westmoreland

The large print giveth, and the small print taketh away.
—musician Tom Waits

A politician will do anything to keep his job—even become a patriot.

—*publisher William Randolph Hearst*

Seen one president, you've seen them all.

—*Henry A. Kissinger*

When a man has cast his longing eye on offices, a rottenness begins in his conduct.

—*President Thomas Jefferson*

The office of President is such a bastardized thing, half royalty and half democracy, that nobody knows whether to genuflect or spit.

—*columnist Jimmy Breslin*

The American presidency, it occurs to us, is merely a way station en route to the blessed condition of being an ex-president.

—*author John Updike*

A straw vote only shows which way the hot air blows.

—*William Sydney Porter (O. Henry),
in* Everybody's Magazine

I think the most un-American thing you can say is, "You can't say that."

—*Garrison Keillor*

Politics is the gentle art of getting votes from the poor and campaign funds from the rich, by promising to protect each from the other.

—*labor organizer Oscar Ameringer*

I believe there is something out there watching over us. Unfortunately, it's the government.

—*filmmaker Woody Allen*

If you see a snake, just kill it—don't appoint a committee on snakes.

—Ross Perot

In our brief national history we have shot four of our presidents, worried five of them to death, impeached one and hounded another out of office. And when all else fails, we hold an election and assassinate their character.

—P. J. O'Rourke

A patriot must always be ready to defend his country against
his government.

—writer Edward Abbey

To announce that there must be no criticism of the president,
or that we are to stand by the president right or wrong, is not
only unpatriotic and servile, but is morally treasonable to the
American public.

—President Theodore Roosevelt

What's the difference between a whore and a congressman?
A congressman makes more money.

—Edward Abbey

The hardest thing in the world to understand is the income tax.
—scientist and thinker Albert Einstein

~

Neither Beltway party is going to drain this swamp, because to them it is not a swamp at all, but a protected wetland and their natural habitat.

—Pat Buchanan

~

Take our politicians: they're a bunch of yo-yos. The presidency is now a cross between a popularity contest and a high-school debate, with an encyclopedia of clichés the first prize.

—*novelist Saul Bellow*

A Democrat sees the glass as half empty. A Republican sees the glass as something that can be made cheaper in China.

—*comic John Higgins*

The American political system is like fast food— -mushy, insipid, made out of disgusting parts of things, and everybody wants some.

—*P. J. O'Rourke*

Voting is simply a way of determining which side is the stronger without putting it to the test of fighting.

—*H. L. Mencken*

In America, with all of its evils and faults, you can still reach through the forest and see the sun. But we don't know yet whether that sun is rising or setting for our country.

—*Dick Gregory*

People used to complain that selling a president was like selling a bar of soap. But when you buy soap, at least you get the soap.

—historian Henry Adams

Politics, as a practice, whatever its professions, has always been the systematic organization of hatreds.

—Henry Adams

Any American who is prepared to run for president should automatically, by definition, be disqualified from every doing so.

—Gore Vidal

A politician is a fellow who will lay down your life for his country.
                    —*saloonkeeper and actress Texas Guinan*

In politics, a lie unanswered becomes truth within twenty-four hours.
                    —*Willie Brown*

I guess I just prefer to see the dark side of things. The glass is always half empty. And cracked, And I just cut my lip on it. And chipped a tooth.
                    —*Janeane Garofalo*

Suppose you were an idiot. Suppose you were a member of Congress. But I repeat myself.

—*author Mark Twain*

When I see flags sprouting on official lapels, I think of the time in China when I saw Mao's *Little Red Book* on every official's desk, omnipresent and unread.

—*author and television producer Bill Moyers*

Hell, I never vote for anybody. I always vote against.

—*comedian W. C. Fields*

The twin disappointments of politics: knowing a candidate is incapable of performing the duties of the office and watching him dance at the inauguration.

—*Martin Higgins*

Man, when you lose your laugh, you lose your footing.

—*author Ken Kesey*

VIII.

LAST
LAUGH

PRESIDENT GEORGE W. BUSH and Secretary of State Colin Powell are sitting in a bar. A man walks over and says, "Wow, this is a real honor. What are you guys doing in here?"

Bush says, "We're planning World War Three. This time we're going to kill a million Iraqis and a blonde with big breasts."

The guy exclaimed, "A blonde with big boobs? Why kill a blonde with big breasts?"

Bush turns to Powell, punches him on the shoulder, and says, "See, I told you. . . . No one would worry about the million Iraqis!"

—*Anonymous*

ACKNOWLEDGMENTS

Without my good friend and editor, Bill K., who labored to pull this diverse material into coherence, I would still be sorting quotes and scribbling fulminations. Thanks to Father Larry Solan and my family at St. Mark Church for their prayers and kindness. Undying gratitude goes to Laura, my loving, long-suffering wife, for her encouragement and optimism, and also to my teen daughters, Brenna and Ayla, for cleaning the kitchen and doing a load of wash.

INDEX